# Can I Have A Dollar?

# Rich Holley

## Illustrated by Sona & Jacob

**BK**
**ROYSTON**
Publishing

BK Royston Publishing LLC
P. O. Box 4321
Jeffersonville, IN 47131
http://www.bkroystonpublishing.com
bkroystonpublishing@gmail.com
502.802.5385

Cover Design: Elite Covers
Illustrated by: Sona & Jacob

ISBN-13: 978-1-959543-05-3

Printed in the USA

# Dedication

I would like to first, thank my amazing wife who has been my driving force to bring the message to everyone.

To my wonderful mother who has been my biggest cheerleader all my life.

It's a sunny summer Saturday afternoon.

Rich is looking out his window.

Suddenly, he sees the ice cream truck coming down his street.

His friends are chasing the truck down the street.

Rich searches all over his room for money.

# In the Piggy bank, nothing.

# In his pants on the floor, nothing!

# Under the bed, that's right, nothing.

Then it happens, Rich asks his Dad for a dollar.

"Please, the ice cream man is outside."

Dad asks Rich,
"Where's the $5 dollars
I gave you last week?"

Rich says,
"I spent it all."

"Ok, then where is the money you got from your mother yesterday?"

# Rich replies, "I spent that too."

Dad says, "Rich I have told you over and over, spend some, save some, so you'll always have some."

With Rich's big brown puppy dog eyes, He says, "Dad please?"

"Ok kid," said Dad.

"Here's $5 dollars and get me an ice cream cone."

Rich smiles and puts $1 in his piggy bank and runs to the ice cream truck with the other $4.

He says, "From now on, I will spend some, save some, so I'll always have some."

# THE END

CPSIA information can be obtained
at www.ICGtesting.com
Printed in the USA
LVHW070407161222
735346LV00009B/167